# The Idea That Is The United States of America:

*Its Occult Foundation*

Etta D. Jackson

All rights reserved. No part of this publication may be reproduced, stored in a retrieval system, or transmitted in any form or by any means, electronic, mechanical, photocopying, recording or otherwise, without the prior permission of the copyright owner.

All inquiries should be addressed to: Etta D. Jackson

Email: arcanum33@gmail.com

Phone: +1 917 667-8511

Website: http://www.ancientmysterybooks.com

International Standard Book No. 0-9746101-6-X

First Edition Published in the United States of America by Lapis Communications

Printed in the United States of America

# Table of Contents

| | |
|---|---|
| Introduction | 1 |
| Author's Note | 5 |
| The Adepts Who Shaped the Vision | 7 |
| Egypt's Connection to the American Ideal | 9 |
| Atlantis the Prototype of the American Government | 16 |
| The Fate of Atlantis | 18 |
| Francis Bacon's Implementation of the Plan for New Atlantis | 19 |
| The Order of the Quest—the Adepts Behind the Plan | 25 |
| In Search of the Promised Land | 26 |
| The Role of Rosicrucians in the Founding of the United States of America | 34 |
| The Great Seal— Decoding Its Symbols | 35 |
|     1. The Arms | 36 |
|     2. E pluribus Unum | 36 |
|     3. Anuit Copetis | 36 |
|     4. Novous Ordo Seclorum | 37 |
|     5. Symbolism of the Obverse | 38 |
|     6. Symbolism of the Reverse | 44 |
| The Capstone and the New World Order | 46 |
| End Notes | 48 |
| About The Author | 51 |
| Notes | 52 |

# INTRODUCTION

'The Idea That is the United States of America', is a chapter from my third book: "The Role of Consciousness in Governance", which I chose to highlight in an e-book as I felt this information about the United States of America is very poignant and impactful to everyone, not just those living in the United States America but throughout the world due to the unique cosmic destiny of this country.

The purpose for writing this and all my books is to make the Arcane Mysteries current. To help my audience remember the truth that abides in each individual's soul: that we are divine, we are one, and our destinies are all intertwined. Each person will connect with these works at the level most appropriate for him or her.

In this regard, I would like to direct your attention to the symbols that communicate who and what the United States of America is, and the role it is destined to play in the transformation of itself first, and ultimately the world.

Looking closely at the Great Seal of the United Sates of America, it displays many occult symbols. Most obvious is the unfinished pyramid with reference to Gizah and the country of Egypt.

It is said that the first democratic government that existed was in Ancient Egypt and Akhnaton was its leader. He was described as a very young Priest-King and Pharaoh of Ancient Egypt, who exemplified social consciousness in the administration of a great nation. He saw every living thing as having a Divine right to live well, to hope, and to aspire in a world governed by brotherly love. Described as the first pacifist, the first realist, the first monotheist, the first democrat, the first heretic, the first humanitarian, the first internationalist, the first person known to attempt to found a religion, and was thought to be born several thousand years before histime.

This is the blueprint on which the United States government was founded. Akhnaton, like the emerging group of adepts and initiates who make up the Fifth Kingdom of God- Men, represent the radiant floating capstone or tetrahedron of divine fire on the Great Seal that will complete the masonry of the pyramid.

This same group of enlightened men and women embody the New World Order and are a new species of humans on the planet, who through their upward climb from the valley of human suffering, have achieved liberation and are made wise by the ascent to the mountaintop of spiritual attainment.

They are the guardians of the Race of Man who have guided humanity's evolution. They are now stepping forward to take their positions externally in the differentsystems, departments and institutions of both the public and privatesectors.

The United States of America has been described as the strong child of Europe established through the efforts of the six esoteric orders of Germany, Ireland, France, Scotland, The Netherlands and England.

It was to Francis Bacon, the great mystic from England, however, that the vision for the establishment of the philosophic empire called the New Atlantis, was given. Together with members from these and other countries, the Idea that we call America came to be born in North America.

This 'American Idea' began as far back as two thousand years B.C.; the Mystical Orders of Egypt were aware of the existence of the great western continent called America, and decided that it should be the site of this philosophic empire.

It was also Bacon's conviction that the "Order of the Quest" should be set up in the divinely assigned land of America, which he called the New Atlantis, and that the vision and philosophy of the Quest was to be the foundation upon which the American Republic should be built.

The destiny of this nation, with an Aquarian soul, will see the unfoldment of its people bring about a new age of humanity in which Service, Synthesis, Brotherhood, the restoration of the Feminine to equal power and rulership, and Masonry will be hallmarks.

To America is entrusted the task of making this a reality for its people and then to become a model to the world.

# AUTHOR'S NOTE

I oftentimes feel intuitively that I was present at the time of the founding of the United States of America. On a soul level, I have a deep knowing of the awesome idea that gave birth to this great nation often referred to as "A Beacon on a Hill"— a model for how all countries can evolve and, as with the individual, pass through the stages of: youth, adulthood and old age continuously increasing in knowledge and wisdom. The imperfections of the country reflect those of each person's journey one that begins in ignorance and end in illumination. One of the steps necessary to achieving this is continuous honest self-reflection and self assessment with the aim of fulfilling the destiny of the soul.

Many speak of the United States as a country too young to inform older nations. However, this young country was established under divine direction withspecific guidelines for the enlightenment of its people and theworld.

The United States of America is a representation of peoples of every kindred, tongue and nation. Peoples who like the symbolic 'Prodigal Son' spoken of in all major religions, came to understand that once attaining a certain level in the development of their consciousness, must leave the comfort of home and embark on a journey that would take them to distant lands on foreign shores to expand their consciousness by meeting those who live life differently.

They, like Buddha and the Prodigal Son, yearned for greater knowledge which could not be acquired by staying home. These are the advanced souls from every continent who landed on the shores of America to seed the Aquarian ideas of: Brotherhood, Synthesis and Oneness. It is no wonder that astrologically, the United States of America has an Aquarian soul which provides for the capacity to attain these goals of the Brotherhood of Man, Synthesis and Oneness.

What will also become increasingly evident is that this country was founded on the occult principles laid out in the Masonic legend, which will become the *religion* of this New Age. It is only within this philosophic framework, can the barriers and boundaries separating all segments of humanity be dissolved.

The United States of America is on tract to fulfilling its destiny under the guidance of, and direction of the Adepts and Initiates who have worked in the background to ensure the success of the Divine Plan for this great nation. These Adepts who make up the capstone of the unfinished pyramid seen on the Great Seal of the United States, arethe ones who will finish the work begun eons ago of liberating humanity from the bondage ofignorance.

# The Adepts Who Shaped the Vision

The New World Order as described by Dr. Paul Foster Case in his book: *"The True and Invisible Rosicrucian Order"*, is an order of immortals, whose nucleus is now on this planet. It is composed of the new creatures that constitute a new species of organic life. This book gives the context for how this emerging New Order of the Ages as the next step in the unfoldment of the Divine Plan for Humanity and the World, puts the United States of America at the center of the establishment of the kingdom above on Earth.

It all began with the rise of a democratic dream in Europe, which prompted the beginning of a western civilization, and so those in search of a Promised Land looked west to a virgin continent populated by Indian tribes— a vast continent suitable for the establishment of a democratic commonwealth.

It was well known that in this New Land one could experience freedom from tyranny, intolerance, and enforced poverty, and so by the nineteenth century, the hope of a better life drew streams of immigrants from almost every nation on earth. Here, there were opportunities for education, free enterprise, and a life lived according to the dictates of hope and conscience. Consequently, in a relatively short time, the races had met and mingled, and a new race — the American race, — was born, a race determined and set apart by a conviction; a conviction that human beings are created free and equal, and are entitled to equal opportunities for perfecting their life, their liberty and the pursuit of their happiness, which is not determined by an analysis of one's blood or the proportions of one's cranium.

We have also discovered that the race of democracy is distributed throughout the world among men and women of all nations and all races who share this conviction, and because they do, they too are of the American race. This realization is the mark of the beginning of a world democracy. The old philosophers taught that physical birth was an accident, since men and women born of different nationalities and races were born under the law of generation. The ancients believed that wise men were of a separate race, born through the second birth, which they achieved by the mind having been developed, through proper intent, to a state of enlightened intelligence. Through this second birth, the individual emerged out of any particular race or nation into an international race and an international nation, which is the larger race and nation that will eventually inherit the earth.[1]

# Egypt's Connection to the American Ideal

It is to this international race and nation that Akhanaton, the first democratic leader, who was a child of the second birth, belonged. Akhanaton, the very young Priest-King and Pharaoh of ancient Egypt, is described as the first man in recorded history to exemplify social consciousness in the administration of a great nation. He saw every living thing as having a Divine right to live well, to hope, and to aspire in a world governed by brotherly love.[2] Described as the first pacifist, the first realist, the first monotheist, the first democrat, the first heretic, the first humanitarian, the first internationalist, and the first person known to attempt to found a religion, he was born several thousand years before his time.[3]

To Akhanaton, Aton (God) was not a mighty warrior ruling over Egypt, speaking through the oracles of priests, nor some Supreme Being flying through the air in a chariot leading armies of destruction. To him, Aton was a gentle father who loved all his children, of every nation and race, who desired that they live together in peace and comradeship, and who felt that the social problems faced by humanity were related to religion. He knew that the Aton created all things — from the smallest to the mightiest; that he had fashioned them in his wisdom, and preserved them with his love and tenderness. And so, this Pharaoh traveled alone through the countryside, meeting the peasants, conversing with slaves, and sharing the simple food of the poor.[4]

He listened with great respect, because in each of his subjects he sought and found the life of Aton. He witnessed the Universe shinning through the eyes of little children, and he beheld the beauty of Aton in the bodies of the men who worked in the fields. He could not understand why others failed to see God in everything, as he did. Nor could he accept the inequalities of birth, wealth, or physical estate as justification for men exploiting or persecuting each other. He saw it as his duty, and that of every ruler, to protect the beauty in the hearts of his people, to nourish it and to provide every possible opportunity for its expression and perfection.[5] From his perspective, religious intolerance was impossible among those who worshipped the true Aton, and there was no room for political intolerance in a world governed by the laws of brotherly love, since each individual became the protector and comforter of everyone else, always cherishing the dreams of others equally as he did his own.

*Akhanaton and wife Nefertiti of Egypt*

In his personal life, Akhanaton emerged as the first man in history to bring dignity and gentle beauty to the management of his home.

He was completely devoted to his seven daughters and his wife Queen Nefertiti, whom he always referred to as his beloved wife.

When he died at the age of thirty-six, it was written of him that the spirit with which he died had never been before, and he was indeed, "The beautiful child of the Aton, whose name shall live forever and ever."

*Unfinished Pyramid of the Seal of the USA with Floating Capstone*

This story might help to explain why the capstone, or fire triangle, that the Egyptians call "The Light" appears twice on the reverse of the Seal of the United States of America as the unfinished pyramid; and a radiant triangle, enclosing the all-seeing eye, is another piece of evidence that the structure of government intended by the founders of the American Republic presented itself to their minds as a piece of Egyptian Masonry, as well as the vision and democratic philosophy of the first conscious leader, Akhanaton.[6] The Greeks also knew of the wisdom with which ancient Egypt under Akhanaton flourished, and they wanted to have this influence in the way they governed, so Solon their lawmaker traveled to Egypt to gather information.

In "*The Secret Destiny of America*", Manly P. Hall tells the story of this great Athenian leader, Solon, who visited Egypt in search of the wisdom of Akhanaton. In response to his search, the High Priest of the

Shrine of Sais, who served the Goddess Isis, took him through the long passageways of the temple that led down stone stairs, rutted by time and lit only by flaming torches, to long subterranean chambers hewn out of living rock. A river flowed through the chambers and the High Priest told Solon that this was the sacred Nile which flowed from Egypt through the underworld to water the fields of the immortals.

Accompanied by the Priest and the torchbearers, Solon was rowed out over the dark water in a small black boat that was waiting on the bank of the underground stream. The boat was then anchored on the shores of a tiny island far underground. Two tall columns made of strange metal, which neither rusted nor deteriorated with age, and which were covered with curious writing in an unknown language, glistened in the light from the torches. The High Priest explained the mystery of the columns to an astonished Solon, by pointing a golden rod at the pillars.

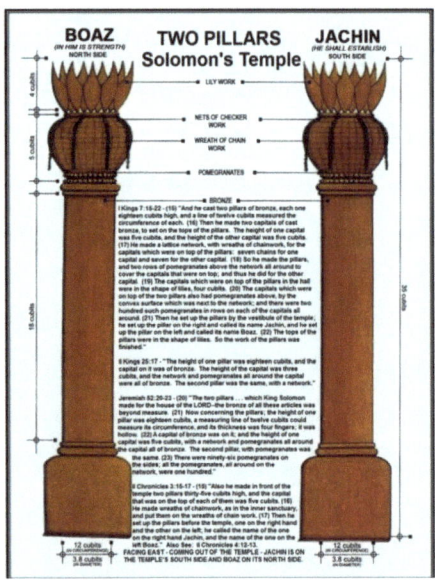

*The Two Columns of Solomon's Temple or the Gateway*

He said that a lost people, who had vanished from the earth, had placed the columns on the island thousands of years ago. He went on to explain that a long time ago a vast empire, whose power extended to every corner of the world, had existed on our planet. Great fleets of merchant ships sailed the seven seas and brought their wealth to its fabulous City of the Golden Gate — the capital of Atlantis. This empire was ruled over by seven kings, descendants of Neptune, the God of the Seas. In this great land there were schools for the study of the mysteries of Nature, towers for the examination of the stars, and, beneath the earth, were mines from which an abundance of precious metals were extracted. Then came the fatal day, when in disobedience to the laws of the gods, the seven kings of the Islands of the west resolved to conquer the whole earth. Prior to this there had been no strife among men, but it was out of this act that war came into being. Coming in great ships from the west, approximately 9000 years before the siege of Troy, the seven kings led an army against the ancient Greeks and invaded Europe.

But before Atlantis sank, its spiritually illumined Initiates, who realized that the land was doomed because it had departed from the path of Light, withdrew from the ill-fated continent, carrying the sacred and secret doctrine with them to Egypt, where they set themselves up as the first Divine Rulers. The world received its heritage of arts, crafts, philosophy, ethics and religion, as well as its heritage of war, perversion and strife as a result. It has been said that through the instigation of the first war, all subsequent wars have been fought in a fruitless effort to justify the first one, and to right the wrongwhich it caused.[7]

This act by the seven kings greatly angered the gods who caused a great earthquake to occur, and the great islands of the West to be submerged into the sea as a result. Sixty million human beings are reputed to have perished because they disobeyed the laws of heaven, and over time even the name of the Atlantic Empire was forgotten, as was the memory of all those who, regardless of their power or wealth, had disobeyed the gods. The High Priest continued to explain: "From these ancient columns, we have read the laws that were given in olden times for the government of nations. These laws are not made by men, but are the will of Eternal Nature. Upon these laws enduring states must be built. To depart from these laws is to die and so perished the nations of the elder world."[8]

These are the pillars of Hercules to which Francis Bacon referred in *Novum Organum* when he indicated that between them runs the path which leads upward from the uncertainties of earth to that perfect order, which is established in the sphere of the enlightened.

In Freemasonry, the two pillars also represent Jachin and Boaz, between which the World Virgin, Isis, — symbol of Nature, — sits; and it also alludes to the fact that Nature attains productivity by means of productivity and that She is the Mother of all productions. As the personification of Wisdom, Isis stands between the pillars of opposites, demonstrating that understanding is always found at the point of equilibrium, and that truth is often crucified between two thieves of apparent contradiction.[9]

*Keeper of the Arcane Mysteries*

Solon returned to Greece with the intention of developing the story of the Atlantic Empire into an epic poem, but due to the responsibilities of the State and the infirmity of age, he failed to do so. However, he told the story to his friend Dropis, who in turn told it to his son Critias. And so, in his 90th year, Critias told the story to his grandson of the same name, who became a disciple of Socrates, which is how the story came to be part of the Platonic dialogues of the samename.

Plato was, first and foremost, a philosopher, and he considered philosophy to be the greatest good ever imparted to man by Divinity. He therefore saw in the account of the fall of Atlantis, the opportunity to summarize his convictions concerning government and politics. Thus, in the Critias, he describes the blessed state of the Atlantean people under the benevolent rulership of ten kings, who were bound together in a league — The Ancient League of Nations. These kings were the monarchs of the seven islands and the three great continents of Europe, Asia and Africa. The ten were said to have been philosopher kings endowed with all virtues, who were wise guardians of the public good, and who obeyed the laws of the Divine Father, Poseidon, — God of the Seas. [10]

# Atlantis the Prototype of the American Government

On one of the columns of the law, it was written that the ten kings of Atlantis should never take up arms against each other for any reason, and that should one break this law, the other nine would unite against him to preserve the peace. Moreover, in all matters relating to the public good, the ten kings were to deliberate together, each being mindful of the just needs of the other. Qabalists attribute this structure and function to the Tree of Life with its ten spheres of Divine emanations, which function as a whole unit, and represent the glyph of Divine Man.

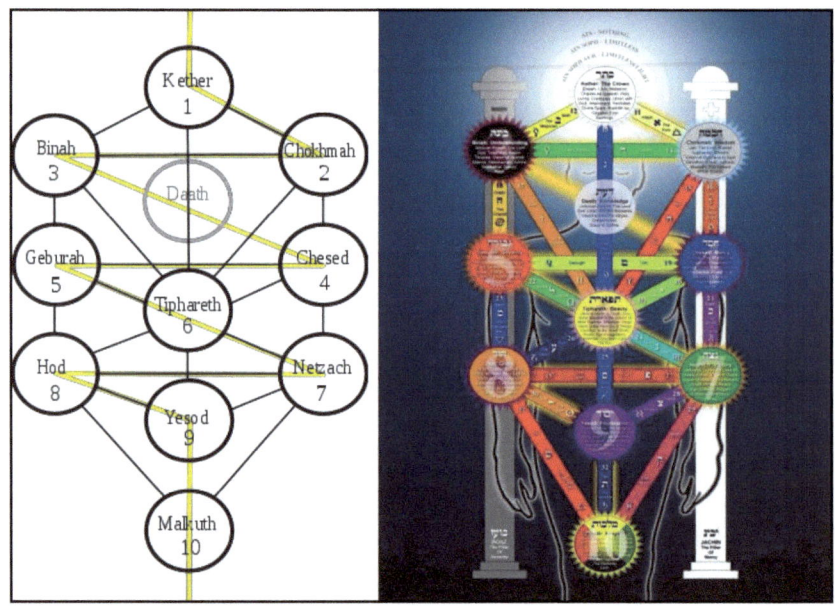

*The Tree of Life- Symbol of Divine Man*

This description of the Atlantean government is a description of the government of the Golden Age, in which men on earth lived according to the laws of heaven. The league of the ten kings is the cooperative commonwealth of mankind; it is the natural and proper form of human government, which is the archetype or pattern of the right government that existed in ancient days, but was destroyed by the selfishness and ignorance of men.

The Critias described how in the beginning of the Atlantean days, wealth and prosperity grew as a result of friendship and sharing, but as the Divine portion of consciousness in them faded away, their souls became diluted with a mortal admixture, and things changed. In the end, as man departed from the perfect pattern and conduct, he denied the very truths which were the foundations of his strength. He lost his spiritual perception, his material ambitions increased, and the desire for conquest was born; as men yearned after that which they had not earned, and gazed with covetous eyes upon the goods of others. Cooperation, Plato states, is natural to the wise, while competition is natural to the ignorant.[11]

Ambition and selfishness caused the dissolution of the league; war came into being, and with it, tyranny, which brought with it oppression, despotism, and the exploitation of people, until finally, the ten kings of Atlantis decided to use their collective power to enslave all the peoples of the earth.[12]

Plato's image of the ideal king is a wise man perfected in the virtues, who is a benevolent ruler of those less informed than himself. This king is a descendant of a Divine Race, belonging to the Order of the Illumined — those who come to a state of wisdom and belong to the family of perfected human beings.[13]

The story of Plato's Atlantis ends with Zeus, — the Ancient of Days, also called Jupiter, God of the thunderbolts, — hurling a thunderbolt against the empire of the sea, shaking it with earthquakes, and destroying it by horrible combustion. The only remaining records were that of vague traditions, and the two columns set up under the temple of Sais, in tribute to Isis.[14]

# The Fate of Atlantis

The destruction of Atlantis can be interpreted, politically, as the breaking up of the ideal pattern of government. So complete was the destruction that in mankind's memory there is no remembrance of a better way of life, and he has therefore accepted the evils of war, crime, and poverty as inevitable. Lost, also, is the world's sense of its own unity. Under a deluge of politics, the perfect state disappeared, and the priest of Poseidon gave way to the priesthood of materialism. Plato's political vision, then, if human beings are to be preserved from their total self-destruction, is for the restoration of the old ways of the Gods, and of the Empire of the Golden Age. Hence, the establishment of the university of Athens —the first school of formal education. At this school men were taught great truths of religion, philosophy, science, and politics, all of which were designed to restore to their minds the vision of the perfect State.

Although old Atlantis was dissolved in a sea of doubts, a philosophic empire would return as a democracy of wise men.

# Francis Bacon's Implementation of the Plan for New Atlantis

Two thousand years later, Francis Bacon restated this vision of a philosophic empire in his book, *New Atlantis*, which describes the model of a college he named "Solomon's House", or the college of the six days work, a thinly veiled reference to the perfection of nature through art.

The six days are the days of creation, as given in the account of Genesis, during which God symbolically created the Universe and brought the natural world into existence.

Likewise, Man, through art, which is philosophy, must create the conditions of his own perfection by means of six philosophic steps. This school is a secret school, the wise man's house in which all arts and sciences are taught according to the Divine understanding of causes, not according to materialistic interpretation.

The college of Solomon's House was comprised of a Society of unknown Philosophers who dwelt together in a gentle commonwealth of scientific and philosophic learning that included the study of medicine, plants and music. It consisted of laboratories, observatories, mines, hospitals and various engines and inventions by which the elements could be controlled and the secrets of nature discovered. In this philosophical city, everyone was employed according to his taste and ability, — each contributing in his own way to the totality of useful knowledge.[15]

In John Heydon's *Holy Guide*, he reprints the New Atlantis as an alchemical allegory, connecting the book of the Rosicrucian Mysteries, by inference, with the symbols of Freemasonry. Bacon writes about "the sons of peace, or of the ladder" as the philosophic empire, called

Bensalem, which existed in the mysterious institution called Solomon's House. Any discerning Mason should be able to see that this Temple or House is that of an order of men and women of universal wisdom and education, all of whom are united in the quest for universal realities.

*Symbol of the Rosy Cruix*

There is every indication that Bacon's dream was for the college of the six days, "Solomon's House", to be erected in America. He strongly felt that this was an area set aside by nature for the perfection of philosophy and the sciences, for the investigation of the laws of life and the mysteries of the universe.[16]

The Ancients held the belief that religion, science, and philosophy are the three parts of essential learning and that any government based on only one or even two of these parts must ultimately degenerate into a tyranny of either men or of opinion.

These three areas comprise the unity of knowledge, and are called: "The Order of the Quest." In this order, religion, which is the quest for truth by means of the mystical powers latent in the consciousness of man, is the spiritual part of learning; philosophy, the quest for truth by the extension of the intellectual powers toward the substance of reality, is the mental part of learning; and the sciences, a quest for truth by the study of anatomy and physiology and of the body of truth, as revealed in the material creation, is the physical part of learning. Together, these three can bring about the perfection of man through the discovery of the Plan for man, because the nature of man is a composite of the spiritual, mental, and physical, which manifests in his daily living.

*Symbol of Solomon's House*

Therefore, if he is to be self-governing, man must become equally informed in all the parts of his nature. The great philosophers of the past were great because they approached the problems of life as priests/philosophers/scientists, knowing that the great secrets of antiquity were the realization of the unity of knowledge. The plan was that an ideal university, — a college of the six day work, would be established in which mankind would learn that the sciences are as sacred as the theologies, and that philosophies are as practical as craft and trades, so that those mystical extra-sensory perceptions viewed with suspicion by the materialists would then be developed according to the disciplines of the sciences.

All learning would then be consecrated to the supreme end of men becoming like gods, and knowing good and evil.[17] Philosophy sets up its house in the world to free men by liberating them from their own excessive desires and ambitions; it saw selfishness as natural to all who are untutored and as the greatest crime against the common good; teaching the completion of the great work of social regeneration, which must be accomplished in man, not in society.

Bacon taught that the democratic commonwealth can never be legislated into existence, nor can it result from formal treaties or conferences, and the Ancient League of Nations was a clear example of this. We saw that the nations which comprised the League, lacked the courage of high conviction, and, therefore, failed the very institution they had established. Bacon believed that permanent progress results from education and not from legislation, since the true purpose of education is to inform the mind in basic truths concerning conduct, as well as the consequences of that conduct.

It should also be clearly understood here that the lesser part of learning is definitely not the fitting of the individual to deal with the problems of economic survival, but instead learning to deal with the intangibles of right motivation and right use, which is the greater part of learning.[18]

In all learning, the fact that the supreme human purpose is the perfection of Man must come first. When this end has been achieved, all good things inevitably follow. No human being, Bacon continues, who is moved to action through wrong motivation or who misuses the privileges of his times, can be considered educated, regardless of the amount of schooling he has received. A human being is established in knowledge through the examples set by leaders and by the personal experiences of living and not by the reading of books alone.

The Baconian system therefore established that there were three sources of learning, namely:

- Learning by tradition, which may be derived frombooks

- Learning by observation, which we learn from the actions of each other
- Learning by experimentation — a study of causes and consequences brought about by personalconduct

Only an enlightened citizenry can sustain enlightened leadership, for only the wise can recognize and reward wisdom; as such, in a democracy, the very survival of the State depends upon the intelligent cooperation of its people.[19]

Solon, the Greek law-giver, declared that an ideal State has few simple laws because they are derived from certainties. By direct contrast, in a corrupt State the laws are many and confused because they are derived from uncertainties, and, like the web of a spider, they catch small insects, while allowing the break-through and escape of the stronger creatures. It was established that where there are too many laws there is lawlessness, and the people come to despise and ridicule the restraints imposed on them. Thus, the degeneration of democracy and the loss of liberty occur when already corrupt laws are amended by further inadequate legislation, revealing the general ignorance of right and wrong. Half-truths, he explained, are the most dangerous form of lies, simply because they can be defended in part by incontestable logic; and since our body of learning has been broken up, those fragments have become partial truths, so that what we are now experiencing is the consequences of division, which must be remedied.[20]

It is a remarkable, fascinating and little known fact that two thousand years before the democracy of 1776, even before the white man arrived, the first American democracy characterized by the spirit of human equality, human cooperation, and freedom of worship, existed and flourished. That democracy was the first League of Nations, created among the Great Lakes Indians of the American Northeast.

Civilization after civilization has been built by human courage and destroyed by human ignorance. We are now at the beginning of a New Age and on the threshold of a day of reckoning. It must be remembered that when humanity willfully ignores the Universal Laws which govern his destiny, Nature has unique and devious ways of pressing home the lessons.[21]

# The Order of the Quest—the Adepts Behind the Plan

In every age, as in this, there is a body of enlightened humans with the intellectual and the spiritual perceptions that are united in what might be termed the *Order of the Quest*. It has been revealed to them that civilization has a *Secret Destiny* — one whose high purpose is not realized by the great mass of people, since they have no knowledge that they are part of a Universal Motion in time and space.

Thousands of years before the beginning of the Christian era, many enlightened thinkers from Egypt, Greece, India, and China discovered that the Will of God is expressed through nature, in the affairs of men. These philosophers knew that world democracy was the secret dream of the great sages, philosophers, seers and mystics like: Aristotle, Pythagoras, Buddha, Jesus, Lao Tse, Mohammed, and Quetzalcoatl.

In pursuit of accomplishing this greatest of human ends, they outlined programs of education, religion, and social conduct directed to ultimately achieve a practical and universal Brotherhood, of which current Masonry is but a faint reflection.

As far back as two thousand years B.C., the mystical orders of Egypt were aware of the existence of the great Western Continent called America, and decided that it should be the site of this philosophic empire.[22]

It was also Bacon's conviction that the *Order of the Quest* should be set up in the divinely assigned land America, which he called the New Atlantis, and that the vision and philosophy of the Quest was to be the foundation upon which the American Republic should be built.

# In Search of the Promised Land

The desire to pillage the treasures of the New World was the overarching motivation of those who sought to colonize the Western Hemisphere; their goal being to amass hordes of gold, and silver, and to build palaces encrusted with jewels. With this in mind, large self-financed expeditions, and others subsidized by the State, set out to exploit the New Land. Spain seemed to have profited the most and so it became clear very early on that only sober colonization would yield the results of a Higher Order.

The western hemisphere was also virgin soil for the Christian faith, whose priests eagerly accompanied the Conquistadores in order to convert pagan tribes and nations to the faith of the old world.

Under the guise of holy inquisition, tens of thousands of Indians were killed, and the Mayans' libraries with all their historical records were destroyed. Over time, the explorers and adventurers brought back reasonably accurate accounts of the natural advantages of the resources of the Americas.[23]

The French and the Dutch set up territories along the Atlantic seaboard, but Sir Francis Bacon, who had given up hope of bringing his dream to fruition in his own country of England, set up the Secret Order in America in the middle of the 17th century.

The Divine assignment was entrusted to him and his genius gave purpose to the whole enterprise. Membership in Bacon's Secret Society was not limited to England, and was most powerful in Germany, France, and the Netherlands. It included most of the leading European thinkers of the time who were involved in the vast pattern of Bacon's purpose. This mystic empire of the wise had no national boundaries, with a citizenry of Alchemists, Qabalists, Rosicrucians, and Mystics of every land who had migrated to the new colony during the early stages of the colonization and set up their organizations in places they found to be suitable.

Paul Foster Case, in his book ***The Great Seal of the United States***, indicates that in the design of the Seal by the first committee, was a coat of arms in six quarters, with emblems representing the countries of: England, Scotland, Ireland, France, Germany, and Holland (The Netherlands), representative of the countries from which the new nation was originally peopled.[24]

Bacon very quickly realized that this new land provided the ideal environment for the establishment and accomplishment of the dream of the philosophic empire. However, he was not alone in this endeavor. He was the head of a secret society, which included in its membership men of high rank and broad influence, who were the most brilliant intellectuals of his day. Bound together by the common oath of labor and the cause of world democracy, they devised the colonization scheme.

Bacon made sure that the American colonists were indoctrinated in the principles of religious tolerance, political democracy and social equality, carefully appointing representatives for a democratic machinery, which was in place for over a hundred years before the Revolutionary War.[25]

Some of the colonizers were of the ***Order of the Quest***, but many were not, and so it was not long before religious strife broke out in the colonies, as much of the intolerance of the old world came over with them to plague the new civilization. It is well known that people do not change their natures merely by changing their place of habitation, and it soon became clear to Bacon and his ***Secret Society*** that not only were they still pioneering in the areas of right thinking and right living, but that much work needed to be done before the philosophic empire would emerge in America.

The country saw many changes in social and political life; cities sprung up and trade flourished, as did most of the important secret societies of Europe and England since with the American organizations under European sovereignty, membership in the two hemispheres were bound together by understanding and sympathy. The plan Bacon had outlined was working out on schedule; quietly and industriously, America was being conditioned to fulfill its destiny of leadership in the free world.

No account of the work of the Secret Societies in America can be complete without highlighting the input of Dr. Benjamin Franklin, a quiet, dignified, scholarly and gentle man who, despite having never been the country's President or a military general, stands out as one of the country's most important figures in the struggle for American independence. Even though he was not a law maker, because of the enormous psychological influence he had on colonial politics, his words became law.

Few knew that the source of his power was the secret society to which he belonged, and for which he was the appointed spokesperson. His profound wisdom was reflected in the Almanac he wrote under the penname, "Poor Richard". He understood the farmer and the philosopher, and knew the languages of both. Franklin spoke for ***The Order of the Quest*** both at home and abroad, especially in France where he received many honors. He watched the New Atlantis take shape, as well as the plan set out by Francis Bacon one hundred and fifty yearsbefore.[26]

*Copy of the Declaration of Independence*

There have been numerous prophetic statements made throughout the centuries foreshadowing the emergence of this great empire. The first president, George Washington, the Flag, and the Great Seal of the United States, could all be seen as emblematic expressions of that profound esoteric document, the ***Declaration of Independence.***

Ancient writings are prolific with the sense of destiny which surrounded this New Land. Among these were predictions made public in 1732 by Sir William Hope, deputy governor of Edinburgh

Castle in his little book on fencing written forty-four years before the Revolutionary War and the United States Declaration of Independence. In it, he foretells the destiny of the United States, and more specifically the awesome responsibility and obligation America has to achieve its liberation and in turn becoming a beacon of light to the world.

At this time the then thirteen colonies had not devised a plan for independence, and George Washington had just been born in Virginia. Of the fifty-six men who signed the Declaration of Independence, twenty were but small boys, and eighteen were not yet born. Little is known of Sir Hope except that his wirings seem to reflect some knowledge of Cabala and Astrology, as well as the specific mention of four men by numbers — George Washington, Abraham Lincoln, Benjamin Harris, and William Mc Kinley, , and the significant occurrences in their lives. Reference is made to the contributions these presidents would make to the United States as well as to the two tombs in which George Washington would be buried and the 555 foot monument to be erected in his honor — the tallest memorial ever constructed to the memory of a man.

*An idea of the first Flag*

The story is told of the committee for the design of the Flag, chaired by Dr. Franklin, which met in Cambridge Massachusetts at the home of the host. Described as a man beyond seventy years old, still in the prime of his life who ate no meat, fish nor fowl, but whose diet was comprised of nuts, ripened fruits, tea, honey and molasses, he was referred to as the "Professor," who spent his time reading ancient manuscripts and pondering over rare books. With the approval of George Washington, the Professor completed the committee of signers, as the seventh person to do so.

After a preamble, it was suggested by Franklin, that the entire committee listen to remarks by this new found and honorable friend who stated:

"The sun of our political air, like the sun in the heavens, is very low in the horizon — just now approaching the winter solstice, which it will reach very soon. But, as the sun rises from his grave in Capricorn, mounts its resurrection in Aries, and passes onward and upward to his glorious culmination in Cancer, so will our political sun rise and continue to increase in power, in light, and in glory; and the exalted sun of summer will not have gained his full strength of heat and power in the starry Lion until our Colonial Sun will be, in its glorious exaltation, demanding a place in the governmental firmaments alongside of, coordinate with, and in no wise subordinate to, any other sun of any other nation upon earth."[27]

He also added that over time the gradual modification of the Flag would be made in order to reflect the new nation gestating in the womb of time. In Cambridge, on January 2, 1776, in the presence of the army, George Washington, with his own hands, raised the newly made flag on a tall, specially made pine, liberty tree pole. The British Army was just as pleased as the Colonies, and gave an official salute of thirteen guns in honor of the newstandard.[28]

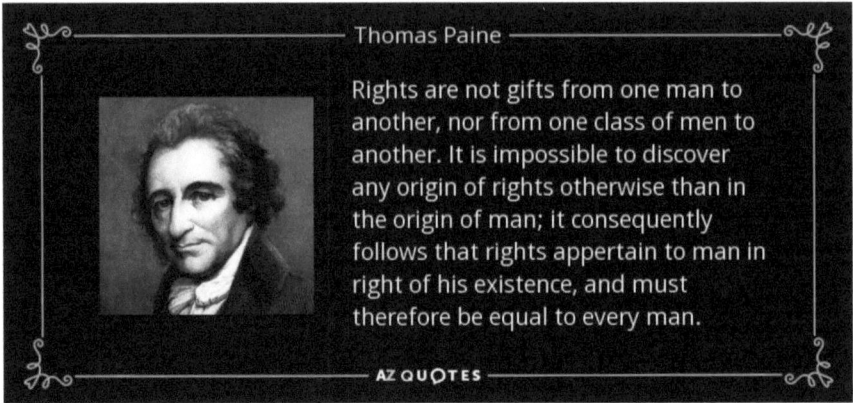

> **Thomas Paine**
>
> Rights are not gifts from one man to another, nor from one class of men to another. It is impossible to discover any origin of rights otherwise than in the origin of man; it consequently follows that rights appertain to man in right of his existence, and must therefore be equal to every man.
>
> AZ QUOTES

Thomas Paine, a Quaker and Englishman by birth, came to America at the suggestion of Benjamin Franklin, and became a great champion in the cause of freedom for the colonies. And it is said that he did more to win the independence of the colonies with his pen, than George Washington accomplished with his sword. The vision he had for the country would require a complete re-organization of the government, religion, and education from its present status. Most people believed that he assisted Thomas Jefferson in the writing of the Declaration of Independence, while others believe that he composed the entire document, and then submitted it to Jefferson who edited and revised it. A free thinker, and a radical pamphleteer, he was considered to be born before his time. However, by his very birth and the nature of his energy, he was able to change the face of time. He emphasized the separation of church and state in his book, ***The Age of Reason***, and believed that when the clergy involved itself in the political conspiracies of the State, it descended to the level of self-interest; he believed that when their spiritual powers were prostituted they would lose all public respect. He witnessed the conniving, plotting, and counter-plotting of religious leaders who had cast their lot in with the aristocracy against the long suffering and exploitedcitizens.

He felt that it was bad enough for government to burden the people with extravagancies, but even worse for the church to preach that men should accept this load as coming from God as being designed to purify their souls through the practice of patience and humility.[29]

Paine was correct in his assessment. As we know, political experience and wisdom lead one to realize that the possibilities of public office are limited and good things are brought about slowly. However, when the dream of world democracy is finally realized, Paine's name and memory will undoubtedly be immortalized.

On July 4th, 1776, fifty-six patriotic men gathered in the old State House in Philadelphia for the solemn purpose of proclaiming the liberty of the American colonies. The names of men like: Benjamin Franklin, John Adams, Thomas Jefferson, John Hancock and a few others are readily recognized, but the majority was unknown men, and to write their history would be to write that of the **Order of the Quest**.

It can be said that it is the mysterious and obscure persons — those who receive little or no credit for the part they play, that further almost all great causes; and in this case, these men were from many nations and cultures. An old book of rules used by the brothers of the Secret Orders reveals the following: "Our brothers shall wear the dress and practice the customs of those nations *to* which they travel, so that they shall not be conspicuous or convey any appearance that is different or unusual. Under no condition shall they reveal their true identity, or the work which they have come to accomplish, but shall accomplish all things secretly and without violating the laws or statutes of the countries in which they work."[30]

Among the unknowns was the ***Professor*** who assisted in designing the Flag.

# The Role of Rosicrucians in the Founding of the United States of America

The Declaration of Independence set forth the veiled principles of Rosicrucianism with careful phrases from the ***Fama Fraternitatis***, a manifesto created in Europe circa 1610 by the Rosicrucian Order. It stated that the coming of: ***The Strong Child of Europe*** who, once it had attained its growth on the American Continent, would be the channel of Freemasonry, and that essentially Rosicrucian ideas would be made the first principles of the ***New Order of the Ages*** as stated in the American Declaration of Independence.[31]

In secrecy and anonymity, well ordered aid was given to the Universal Plan in the struggle for human equity and justice that has been America's destiny throughout the past, and into our present time. This destiny will continue to be served by the unknowns until the Platonic empire is established on the earth, and the two towers of the ***New Atlantis*** rise from the ruins of a materialistic and selfish world.[32]

The Rosicrucians left the Great Seal of the United States of America as an imperishable reminder of their secret activities. Late in the afternoon of July 4th, 1776, the Continental Congress resolved that Dr. Franklin, Mr. J. Adams, and Mr. Jefferson were to form a committee to devise a Seal for the United States of America. This was the same committee, except for Robert R. Livingstone and Roger Sherman, which had drawn up the Declaration of Independence that had been signed at about 2 pm that very afternoon.

# The Great Seal—Decoding Its Symbols

The Congress assembled after dinner, desirous of completing the evidence of the independence of the United States by formally adopting an official sign of sovereignty and a national coat of arms. It was understood by each successive committee that the coat of arms and the seal would be one and the same. On the 20th of June 1782, the secretary for the third committee delivered a report describing the Seal, which read as follows:

**ARMS:** *Paleways of thirteen pieces, argent and glues; a chief, azure; the escutcheon on the breast of the American Eagle displayed proper, holding in his dexter talon, an olive branch, and in his sinister, a bundle of thirteen arrows, all proper, and in his beak a scroll, inscribed with the motto,* **"E Pluribus Unum**.*"33 For the CREST: Over the head of the eagle, which appears above theescutcheon, a glory, or, breaking through a cloud, proper, and surrounding thirteen stars, forming a constellation, argent, on an azurefield.34*

**REVERSE:** *A pyramid unfinished. In the zenith, an eye in a triangle, surrounded with a glory proper. Over the eye these words,* **"Annuit Coeptis**.*" On the base of the pyramid the numerical letters MDCCLXXVI. And underneath the following motto:* **"Novous OrdoSeclorum**.*"35*
*The remarks and explanation are as follows:*

*The Esucutcheon is composed of the chief and pale, the two most honourable ordinaries. The pale pieces represent the Several States all joined in one entire solid compact, supporting a Chief which unites the whole and represents Congress. The Motto alludes to this union.*

*The pales in the arms are kept closely united by the chief and the chief depends upon that Union and the strength resulting from it for its support to denote the Confederacy of the United States of America and the preservation of their Union through Congress. The colours of the pales are those used in the flag of the United States of America: White signifies purity and innocence, Red, hardiness & Valour, and Blue, the colour of the Chief, signifies Vigilance, Perseverance & Justice. The Olive branch and the arrows denote the power of peace & war, which is exclusively vested in Congress. The Constellation denotes a new State taking its place and rank among other sovereign powers. The Escutcheon is born on the breast of an American Eagle without any other supporters, to denote that the United States of America ought to rely on their own Virtue.[36]*

**Reverse:** *The pyramid signifies Strength and Duration: the Eye over it & the Motto allude to the many signal interpositions of Providence in favour of the American Cause. The date underneath it signifies the beginning of the New American Era, which commences from that date.*

*Symbol of Freemasonry*

The concepts of the American government, adopted in 1776, are all set forth in detail in the lectures, dramatized in the rituals, and summarized in the symbols of Freemasonry; prior to this date, the lodges in England and America were the only places where the principles of liberty, equality, and fraternity were explained and practiced. Freemasonry taught that all men were brothers, and, as such, all Masons met as equals, and learned from the many experiences and practical helpfulness each to the other, but most of all it taught the great truth, that all Men are brothers. The founders of the nation drew their inspiration from the doctrines of Pythagoras, Plato, the Egyptian schools in Alexandria, the Qabalists, the Rosicrucians, and the Hebrew and Christian scriptures.

### Symbolism of the Obverse

There are many esoteric interpretations of the Seal. Paul Foster Case in his book ***The Great Seal of the United States***, gives his interpretation of the observe side in which he describes the eagle as an ancient symbol of spiritual vision and the only bird capable of looking directly into the sun. He further states that it is connected with the zodiacal sign of Scorpio, which is the ascendant or rising sign of the United States. In astrology, the sign of Scorpio is said to rule the physical forces and functions in the human body that relate to the reproductive system. These energies must be controlled, re-directed and sublimated before the individual can develop true, higher vision. The eagle as a symbol suggests, then, that spiritual vision is essential to true Americanism, and exemplifies how that vision can be attained.[37]

In the eagle's dexter talon is an olive branch, — a symbol of peace, — with thirteen leaves and thirteen berries. These numbers added together result in the number twenty-six, which in Freemasonry and Qabalistic thought relates to Jehovah. It must be noted that the eagles of the monarchies which preceded the United States carried the symbols of war on the dexter side, and by extension to be concluded that the national arms proclaim the principle that the primary aim of the United States shall be to establish peace. And so, it is for this reason that the eagle faces the olive branch, denoting the idea that any nation which dedicates itself to the establishment of peace dedicates itself to the quest for an ever-increasing knowledge of God, or Jehovah.[38] The arrows in the eagle's left talon represent the power of war. However, arrows are more than emblems of war; they are also symbols of **aim** denoting purpose, will, and intention. The number thirteen in Hebrew is related to "love" and "unity", and whenall these ideas are combined, we could conclude that the cardinal principle of true Americanism is that recourse to arms should be for no other purpose than the maintenance of a just cause, having for its objective the establishment and preservation of unity and love.

The colors Red, White, and Blue, Qabalistically yield the number 103; and the interpretation of, **The Stone of Adam** or **The Perfect Red Stone**, which in Freemasonry, relates to the perfect ashlar or squared stone, — symbolic of perfected humanity. This number, which relates to the colors in both the flag and the shield, is a number considered to be related to the Ancient of Days, and refers to the Divine protection, under which the country exists. It also signifies "Builders", or "Masons" and therefore the national colors spell out, by Goematria, the name of the fraternity, which did so much for the American Cause.

Case further states that the dexter wing of the eagle has thirty-two feathers, which is the number for the Paths of Wisdom, and is the summary of the Qabalistic philosophy, as well as the number of ordinary degrees in Scottish Rite Freemasonry.[39]

The sinister wing has thirty-three feathers, and corresponds to the thirty-third degree of the same, conferred on Masons for outstanding service.

The total number of the feathers is sixty-five, which means "together in unity", and is the expression used in the first degree of the Masonic ritual. These are the same ideas expressed by the motto: "***E Pluribus Unum***", which also contains thirteen letters, and suggests that true Americanism cannot be understood to mean rule by the many, as a false definition of democracy implies. Such rule is but the tyranny of the mob, and it is for that reason that the motto indicates a move away form the hydra-headed multifariousness of clashing opinions and toward a singleness of purpose and effort based on real knowledge of the One, from which all things proceed, in other words — a movement of the mind away from the many-ness of external appearance towards the idea of Oneness. This idea has been rejected by academics in the fields of science and philosophy, but today the field of physics accepts this postulate; a concept that has always been an assumption of Qabalistic and Hermetic thought, and which has been the source for the ideals of the founders of the United States — that all things are from OneReality.[40]

The crest over the eagle's head includes a golden glory, an azure field, and thirteen silver stars. Gold represents the Sun; azure the sky-father, the god of thunder and Jupiter who is the Master of the Lodge above.

The constellation of silver refers to the letter "G", seen in most Masonic temples, and refers to the Hebrew word, Gimel, which represents the High Priestess, who sits between the two pillars of Solomon's temple. The constellation of thirteen stars is composed of pentagrams arranged in such a way to form a hexagram, — a symbol of Solomon's Seal, known throughout eternity to represent the forces of the macrocosm, or the "kingdom of the heavens." These forces influence all things in manifestation and all the cycles in and through which they manifest. The pentagram is another symbol of the perfected ashlar, or perfected man, whose mind in this state has dominion over the elements.

*The Hexagram-As Above, So Below*

Surrounding the constellation is a golden glory divided into twenty-four equal parts, a Masonic reference to the twenty-four-inch gauge, emblematic of the twenty-four hour day, which is divided in three equal parts of eight hours each. This is the number of Jesus or Joshua, who succeeded Moses in liberating the children of Israel from Pharaoh and from the bondage to form, or matter.[41]

Behind the azure background are twenty-six horizontal lines —, the number name of Jehovah and another reference to the Master of the Lodge above. Around the glory are nineteen clouds, a reference to

Eve, who all major religions know as the Cause of Form that brought Spirit into Matter, and through the veiling of the One Light, manifests it into matter. The right foundation by which one becomes a doer is symbolized on the obverse Seal by the nine feathers of the eagle's tail. The number nine represents Basis, Foundation or Yesod, which adds to eighty, and is also the number of the Tower, a symbol of Mars, the ruler of the sign of Scorpio, the ascendant of the United Sates, and the energy which must be transmuted so that the United States can grasp a higher vision of its destiny. The number nine also refers to the control of the Martian forces necessary to accomplish the goal.[42]

The combination of the numbers comprising the nineteen clouds, the nine tail feathers, and the twenty-four divisions of the glory, total fifty-two (4x13), which is the number of "Ben" —, the Son, the Christos or Jesus. This is the Mystical Son and universal light- energy made flesh, the one who dwells among us, and is the central point ofillumination personified as Horus in the Egyptian rituals. He is the Word or Logos made flesh and the power whereby all things are made possible. Today, this truth is a fundamental postulate of science and one which Qabalists, Hermeticists, Rosicrucians, and Freemasons in the eighteenth century understood as that single energy, like light in its essential nature, which is the underlying power expressed in every kind of vital activity.[43]

The Declaration of Independence implies what the Seal symbolizes Qabalistically and Hermetically,— that the basis of what the Founding Fathers fought for, is **Truth**. That **Truth** is that the underlying law of the universe is the law of liberty. Mankind is at present enslaved to materialism, but the hour is striking when a revolution greater than that of 1776 is at hand. This revolution will not involve armies, but will be one of consciousness, involving the human soul, a revolution where the shackles of hateful servitude will be thrown off and the false standards of value will be overturned.

Prophets have foreseen this time, but their visions have been ignored, misunderstood, and disregarded. However, the perfect law of liberty is now being more and more greatly realized in the affairs of men.[44]

In ***The Secret Destiny of America***, Manly P. Hall insists that the bird drawn by the designers was the Phoenix. This selection could be understood to reflect the evolutionary process of the United States, as it rises out of the ashes of its transformation, since, as with everyone who passes through the gates of initiation, one must die and become twice-born. This bird of ancient symbolism is the same in size and shape as the Eagle and is described as having a body of glossy purple feathers, with the plumes in the tail being alternately red and blue. The head is light in color with a circlet of golden plumage, and a crest of feathers of brilliant colors at the back of the head. Its home is reputed to be in the distant parts of Arabia, in a nest of frankincense and myrrh. It is said that at any given time only one of these birds is alive and that it lives for 500 years, with its body opening up at death, thus allowing for the emergence of the newborn Phoenix. For this reason, the Phoenix is considered to be representative of immortality and resurrection. It is one of those symbols with tangible origin; one of the signs of the secret order of the ancient world and especially of the initiates of those orders who are considered twice-born. The wisdom conferred by the process of Initiation constitutes a new life. The Phoenix, as a symbol, is emblematic of royalty, power, superiority and immortality, and, in meaning, is identical to the Phoenix in China, Egypt, and Greece as well as to the Thunder Bird of the American Indians.

But, whatever the bird on the obverse side of the seal is, it is nevertheless clearly the stamp of the "Order of the Quest", and in that same context, the reverse of the Seal is irrefutably even more so related to the Ancient Mysteries.[45]

### *Symbolism of the Reverse*

This side of the seal displays the Pyramid of Gizah, believed by the Egyptians to be a shrine to the gods Thoth and Hermes who are personifications of Universal Wisdom. It is composed of thirteen courses of masonry, showing seventy-two stones, and is without a capstone. Its upper platform floats a triangle containing the All-Seeing Eye, surrounded by rays of light. The thirty foot square platform shows no evidence of ever containing a capstone. This is an appropriate symbol since it is representative of human society itself — i.e. unfinished and incomplete. The converging, ascending angles and faces of the pyramid represent the common aspiration of humanity; the radiant triangle with its All-Seeing Eye that floats above is the symbol of the esoteric orders. The triangle is in the shape of the Greek letter Delta, the first letter of the name of God, who is the Divine part of nature that completes the works of men. The Pyramid could, therefore, be called the Universal House with its unfinished apex, or — the Great Architect of the Universe.

In the legend of old Atlantis it is said that a great University stood in its center in the shape of an immense Pyramid, with an observatory at the top of it, for the study of the stars. This temple is shadowed in the seal of the New Atlantis. The question then is: Was it the old philosophers who sealed the new nation with the eternal emblems, so that all nations might know the purpose for which the new country was founded. [46] Case describes the symbolic statement of the reverse seal as displaying the essentials of true Americanism and as a marvel of ingenuity. The upper motto: Annuit Coeptis, like E Pluribus Unum, of the Observe, contains thirteen letters. The date on the lower course of masonry of the pyramid contains nine letters and is in the same position as the nine tail feathers of the bird on the Obverse side of the Seal. The motto: Novus Ordo Seclorum, meaning "the New World Order", contains seventeen letters, and these three together total thirty-nine, or 13 x 3. Qabalistically, the numbers, words and names repeatedly speak to the Divine destiny for which this great nation was brought into manifestation. A further comprehensive look at the esoteric interpretations of the reverse seal can be found in Paul Foster Case's treatise, "The Great Seal of the United States."

# The Capstone and the New World Order

The motto: **Novous Ordo Seclorum** — the New World Order — is represented by the capstone, which completes the unfinished structure depicted on the seal; and the foundation of the work, which will complete and perfect the New World Order, which must be the recognition of the Christos in every human heart. This work must proceed from the principle summed up in the meaning of the name Jesus, — the nature of reality is to liberate. The New World Order must begin with the principle set forth in the words of the Declaration of Independence, which states that the laws of Nature, and of God, are but variations of the one basic law of liberty. In the end, the real nature of the New World Order at the bottom of the reverse seal is that the wise men, who established the republic, knew the time would come when the work of the men represented by the unfinished pyramid, would have to be completed by a power higher than that possessed by ordinary men.

It is only when the individual "stones" of the temple of government,— the persons composing the body political, awaken to the truths so clearly set out in the Declaration of Independence and in the symbolism of the Seal, that we shall see the completion of the structure began in 1776.[47]

America is in great need of a vision of its purpose As each age comes into manifestation, it brings with it definite philosophic revelations of thought designed to solve the problems peculiar to that age, and to help bridge the ethical intervals between generations. This age demands a doctrine of synthesis and a government founded on the philosophy of mutual understanding, where the black and the white, the Jew and the Gentile, the Chinese and the Turk have a fundamental premise of one denominator on which all can agree.

Humanity has become so advanced and strong that it would be dangerous to allow its parts to remain fragmented. We can no longer maintain our position of isolated individualism without endangering the rights of all men.

Democracy is the realization of the unity of life, and in this realization, all competitive standards of civilization which are based on the erroneous assumption that one part of life can survive without, or at the expense of the other, is shattered, because it is upon the basis of competition that the whole structure of human sorrow is erected.[48]

The destiny and the plan devised in secrecy so long ago in far places, upon andabove the earth, were brought into manifestation to be fulfilled openly as the greatest wonder born out oftime.

May Light be Extended Upon You

# End Notes

[1] Hall, Manly P., *The Secret Destiny of America*, Los Angeles: The Philosophical Research Society, 1991, p. 28

[2] Ibid, p. 28

[3] Ibid, p. 32

[4] Ibid, p. 33

[5] Ibid, p. 34

[6] Case, Paul Foster, *The True and Invisible Rosicrucian Order*, Los Angles: Builders of the Adytum, Ltd., 1989, p. 88

[7] Hall, Manly P., *Secret Teachings of All Ages*, Los Angeles: The Philosophical Research Society, 1991, p. 85

[8] Ibid, p. 55

[9] Ibid, p. 130

[10] Hall, Manly P., *The Secret Destiny of America*, Los Angeles: The Philosophical Research Society, 1991, p.57

[11] Ibid, p. 60

[12] Ibid, p. 62

[13] Ibid, p. 59

[14] Ibid, p. 63

[15] Ibid, p. 115

[16] Hall, Manly P., *Lectures on Ancient Philosophy*, Los Angeles: The Philosophical Research Society, 1991, p. 462

[17] Ibid, p. 197

[18] Ibid, p. 193

[19] Ibid, p. 194

[20] Ibid, p. 195

[21] Ibid, p. 197

[22] Hall, Manly P., *The Secret Destiny of America*, Los Angeles: The

Philosophical Research Society, 1991, p.25

[23] Ibid, p. 128

[24] Case, Paul Foster, *The Great Seal of the United States,* Los Angles: Builders of the Adytum, Ltd., 1989, p. 3

[25] Hall, Manly P., *The Secret Destiny of America*, Los Angeles: The Philosophical Research Society, 1991, p.130

[26] Ibid, p. 134

[27] Ibid, p. 152

[28] Ibid, p. 154

[29] Ibid, pp. 159-161

[30] Ibid, p. 172

[31] Case, Paul Foster, *The True and Invisible Rosicrucian,* Los Angles: Builders of the Adytum, Ltd., 1989, p.150

[32] Hall, Manly P., *The Secret Destiny of America*, Los Angeles: The Philosophical Research Society, 1991, p. 172

[33] Case, Paul Foster, *The Great Seal of the United States,* Los Angles: Builders of the Adytum, Ltd., 1989, p.4

[34] Ibid, p. 4

[35] Ibid, p. 4

[36] Ibid, p. 5

[37] Ibid, p. 13

[38] Ibid, p. 15

[39] Ibid, pp. 15-16

[40] Ibid, p. 16

[41] Ibid, p. 18  [42] Ibid, pp.20-21  [43] Ibid, p. 22

[44] Ibid, p. 22

[45] Hall, Manly P., *The Secret Destiny of America*, Los Angeles: The Philosophical Research Society, 1991, pp.176-177

[46] Ibid, pp. 179-180

[47] Case, Paul Foster,*The Great Seal of the United States,* Los Angles:

Builders of the Adytum, Ltd., 1989, pp. 31-32.

[48]Hall, Manly P., *Lectures on Ancient Philosophy*, Los Angeles: The Philosophical Research Society, 1991, pp.470-476

# ABOUT THE AUTHOR

Etta Jackson is the founder of the non-profit organization The Institute for Conscious Global Change (ICGC). and has previously authored Understanding Your Choice, Unveiling the Secrets of the Feminine Principle and The Role of Consciousness in Governance. She holds M.S. degrees in Counseling and Administrative Leadership and Psychoanalytic Guidance and Counseling and has one daughter and a grandson.

ETTA D. JACKSON

# NOTES

www.ingramcontent.com/pod-product-compliance
Lightning Source LLC
Chambersburg PA
CBHW041812040426
42450CB00001B/3